Listening from the Inside

By: Michelle Duell Wagner
Psychic Medium
The Saratoga Spiritualist

Kerry,
    Its alway a
pleasure seeing you!
Best wishes!
Michelle Wagner
The Saratoga Spiritualist

<u>Dedication</u>

This book is dedicated to all of the people's lives that have touched mine by sharing and trusting me with the honour of mentoring and reading for you. Crying together because you were able to find peace and also seeing   each of you flourish and grow, will stay in my heart and soul always.
This book is part of me, my legacy that I wanted to share with the world. It is a piece of my life that I hope will encourage you to be true to yourself and know "You are Special, I believe in you and never stop learning ."
  Just as I am learning everyday!

.

Special Thanks to my father Timothy Duell, who always told me I could do anything I put my heart into. Thank you Dad I love you!
To my Mother Constance Duell for finally understanding my gifts. In Memory of Grammy & Pop Riccio, who I know have been with me every step of the way.
To my Husband Scott Wagner for dealing with my moody Psychic Author moments and always bringing me Chocolate. XOXO
To Stephanie Duell my editor and 2nd mom. For all your encouraging chats and wishing for you to follow your dream and write your story now!
Blessings of love and happiness always ~ Michelle

Editors notes

First let me say that being the first to read this book and being asked to edit for Michelle, is one of the greatest opportunities I've had... Understand while I have always believed in psychic awareness as a gift from God delivered by the Angels. I never thought of it as something everyone possesses. I now do!

Studying and working with Michelle has opened me to many realizations. We all have psychic awareness clearly in sync with our ability to believe. I have had a great awakening to psychic awareness and contacting "the other side". Michelle's guidance as an intuitive teacher flows so naturally.

As a matter of fact, I have a testimony to my own experience. While I was spending a lot of time reading and editing I had a "vision or visit".

One day at my bathroom vanity, I clearly felt and saw a woman dressed in the late 1800 early 1900 era white dress. (don't know who she is) She was standing in the doorway smiling at me like a child or loved one looks on. She was gone as quickly as she came and smiled. Then a few weeks later I was leaving work in the evening in a dark parking lot partially full of only empty cars. Suddenly I hear a dogs friendly bark, Be certain there were no dogs anywhere near by. As I got in my car I realized it was the third anniversary of our dog Beau's passing, Immediately I knew this was a greeting from the other side, Hi Mom from Beau.

I believe because I was working so closely with Michelle's work I was open to the vision and visit. I look forward to many more.

As you read this book, open your mind and heart to all possibilities. Remember to "Listen from the inside!"
  Editor; Stephanie Duell

Testimony

By: Ray 'Annie' Boyer Bradley
From: Nebraska

My name is Ray Ann Boyer, however my Momma always called me "Annie Suzy" as I grew up. Annie is what ended up sticking with me my whole life. Michelle and I first met almost 22 year ago. Like Michelle I also had a mixed upbringing. I was baptized in a Christian church, confirmed in a Methodist church, and then became a member of an Evangelical Covenant church. Currently, I do not attend any churches.

I believe in God, but always felt there was more ... I have been blessed to have crossed paths with Michelle and to be mentored by her for many years now.

Her psychic abilities are nothing short of amazing and the way she teaches is almost like talking to a life long friend. She can be tough and does make you work but the there is no end result as she has taught, we never stop learning!

You might wonder how someone can make such a difference in one's life? I, like many people, have always possessed a gift. A gift that many are afraid to talk about. Afraid to be judged; afraid to be labeled as crazy; afraid of the gift itself. Michelle helped me to understand this gift...the gift of psychic ability. The first time she met me withing 10 minutes of meeting she said "You have a Gift". I was amazed because I never told anyone about my experiences and here someone I just met was able to pick up on. Michelle said she read my Energy!

I have always felt presences around me from childhood days. These feelings became stronger as I aged. I never understood my feelings and pushed them aside. I would feel a touch; only to turn around to find nothing there.

I dabbled in books about witchcraft, gods and goddesses when I was younger, which led me to question whether other things or abilities indeed existed? This always peeked my own curiosity even as a adult. I had always believed in the spiritual world, but was terrified to actually talk to anyone about it. But, then Michelle and I connected. Though states and many miles separated us, our friendship was born. She had an understanding of me and wasn't afraid to tell me that I did indeed have "a gift." We spent many hours talking on the phone, as she explained and assisted me in understanding my psychic abilities, the energies of the universe, and how these things connected within me. I no longer needed to push these feelings aside.

  Since then, I have had numerous incidences, including spirits that have communicated to me through touches and one actual apparition appearing.

Animal spirits, namely dog spirits, have connected with me. My gift has been opened up because of Michelle and her methods. Here's to many more conversations, and experiences to be shared... I love and admire you, and your beautiful soul. You are a gift that needs to be shared with the world. Please use this book as I will. This is a tool that will help my daughters and grandchildren someday.

I now can pick up in others if they have Gifts, just like Michelle did with me. I am still an existing student and friend after so many years.

I am honored to give this testimony of my own personal experiences with Michelle as my Mentor and using the Methods in "Listening from the Inside"

Annie

About the Author (About Me)

When I was only 5 years old I realized I was different. I could not only see but hear dead people. Now I know what you're going to say ...So typical of a Psychic/Medium. But this was in 1975!! Anyone who was born in the 70's knows that saying out loud or even talking about being different, or having abilities was not as open as we are today. Back then, the only people that I talked about what I was experiencing was my father, grandmother and mother. My mother was actually scared to death from some of the things I was saying.

I was born into a Roman Catholic Family, on my mothers' side was 100% Italian and practiced Strega. If you do not know what

Strega is, it is Italian hereditary White Witch Craft. The Strega part did not come until a little later in life, but the Catholic part was from birth. I was Baptized, went to Catechism on Sundays, made my Communion and conformation in the Catholic Faith. All mind you while also being a Strega, and a Psychic/Medium. I confided in my Grandmother a lot and spent a lot of time in nature with my father. I had a wonderful childhood and would not change it for the world. It was a very different time being a kid then. I remember being outside a lot and using my imagination or so I had thought it was my imagination back then. I remember spending a lot of time in a cemetery that sat on a hill, over a creek behind my house. For some reason I felt at peace when I was there. My dear friend Beth, my brother Mitch and I, would sit for hours in that cemetery. On the other side of course made for the best Sleigh riding, Happy Memories!

I have furthered my studies as I grew up and realized what I am; I am now, a Reiki Master, an Ordained Minister, and have a doctrine in Meta-psychics. I am the Lead Psychic/Medium for the Extreme Paranormal Encounter Response Team (E.X.P.E.R.T.) We do investigate a lot of well know haunted locations to build the core strength of our Team, and we take on private cases. It helps build trust in one another.

Some of my favorite Investigations are Daniel Klaes Haunted Hinsdale House, which I am looking forward to visiting again in the Summer of 2018. Rolling Hills Insane Asylum, and the Bergen House Investigation hosted by

Ted Van Wolf that Tim Conwell & I ventured in on. Also a special Thanks to Ted Van Son for giving me the honor being the resident Psychic on Ted's Podcast show "Paratalk Radio".

I have studied many religions, both practiced in Churches, and in nature. Including Pagan, Wiccan, Hoo-doo, Voo-doo, Shaman, American Indian and many more. My point to anyone reading my book is.... I do not need to list all these studies or titles after my name. I am Michelle Duell Wagner and I am a Psychic Medium. I have been blessed with many gifts. That I would love to share with as many people as possible.

I believe that these gifts are not only from God, but from The Goddess, Nature, The Sun, Moon, Stars and the Universe. I am beyond grateful for having the life that I have had and show gratitude to everyone and everything.

Was my life always easy? "NO IT WASN'T" but I knew it was something I had to get

through to get me to the next step, which I always had hoped would be better than the last. Please enjoy the book, use it as a tool to help you develop your gifts, no matter what they are and always believe in yourself! Blessings to each of you on your Journey!
Michelle Duell Wagner

Chapter 1 ~ Listening from the Inside

Have you ever Listened to people from the inside? Listened sooo close, you can hear their thoughts and all their memories ...Hear them think from places they do not even know they could think from?

This is the beginning of how to open your Personal Psychic Intuition and gifts that I feel everyone is born with. My concept is that, every person can receive communication this way. Making contact with these gifts will expand your intuition, develop your gifts, lead to you achieving your personal goals, and assist you in personal and professional ways. This includes everyone who is just trying to revisit their wonderings or open a natural block that happens as we all grow up. It can be as simple as remembering things you were able to do with your gift when you were a child.

Unless you are encouraged to talk about them or find a way to express exactly what you may have been seeing, hearing, feeling no matter your age. It can be frustrating. Documenting your stepping stones is very important no matter what age you start and can been done in a variety of ways.

Having someone in your life that will record or remind you of these sometimes hidden talents really does help later in life when you try to revisit the things your gift allowed you to do at different levels of Natural development of your Psychic Awareness. But that is not saying you can not start now!   So please, do not feel discouraged if you do not have any of these memories saved. The reason why is, I can tell you I bet you do!

It could be a picture you colored as a child, a sketch you doodled as a teen, even a number you wrote down on your grocery list. These little things that we don't know why we save, you will learn why you really did! Continuing to develop your gift and learning the many benefits and rewards that come into your life daily is a true blessing. So please remember no matter how small, show gratitude always.

The first thing I would like you to do is please get yourself a journal. I never used anything fancy. Just a notebook will do to start and you can always invest in more expensive tools later. My goal is to show everyone that you do not need to go out and buy this or that to achieve what you are after. "Listening From YOUR inside" cost's us nothing but time and some dedication.

If you have the honor of having older family members still living spend some time with them. A lot of people do not realize until it is too late that our elders hold a lot of knowledge. They lived in a very different age then we are in now. They can help you to remember the things I mentioned that you may have done when you were younger. They may even tell you how much you reminded them of someone else in your family that you never knew, but have some of the same habits, likes, dislikes and personality traits. This is such a gift in itself, just like a Family Tree this may tell you where your gift derived from. You may already know where you may have inherited part of your gifts from, but everyone and every generation always has something just a little different than the last. I know this from my own family . I also know that some of my talents are just my own. That is the magic of being you. You have a unique blue print that makes you different without even adding in an extra Psychic Sense.

In future lessons of the book are proven methods from my own personal experiences and also those whom I have mentored. Not everyone learns the same just like everyone gifts are not the same . Yes, we can categorize them to help develop them, but each of you will make my educational tools your own.

For me I was fortunate that I had a loving support system in my parents and grandparents that knew how to help me keep this open in me. Was it an easy task? Nope! Not at all. I do owe a lot of my wanting to continue this path to them and can't express how grateful I am. Everyone has some part of a blockage even if it isn't on a psychic side. It could also be a emotional block. Something that happened in your life where you may have trusted your gut feeling or instinct and it turned out not to be correct and you got hurt from it. I can not tell you how many times through the years I have learned that this is where "Listening from the Inside" has become muted and not clear. It happens to us all. Even to me!   But I used it as a learning process. To try to figure out WHY it didn't work?   I did and still am expanding this knowledge even as I am writing this book for you. But this is why I am sharing it with you now and not later because I feel you truly never stop learning and there are NO MASTERS in this field. We all just do things our own way. Carving our own paths to what we want to do with our own Gifts.

This process that I present to you is an ever growing process that will help you in weeks and months. Not the many years that it has taken me to test them. This is not me making something up. This is me explaining the best way I can, from my own trails and errors. I developed methods by myself to mentor and teach many students in my life to begin to reopen something they were born with.

Life can be messy and putting up a mental block to protect ourselves from heart break, being hurt, letting someone else make decisions, for you, all can all hinder your natural gift from taking its full potential. This is the easiest way for people to protect themselves in the everyday world. But you are not an everyday person. YOU ARE SPECIAL. When we get frightened or may not have control as much as we like over our gifts this can also cause a blockage. But to truly want more, you also have to learn how to open up more and learn how to properly protect yourself and your energy too.

When we are children the possibilities are endless. We have really no responsibilities except developing our minds as we grow. With this a lot of imagination, hope, and a little magic happens. This is almost where we need to get back to reopening the innocent imagination and beliefs of endless hope, playfulness and true believing in what we feel in faith in   ourselves and others.

  At some point our parents tell us, its time to go to bed, time to get up and get ready for school, time to do your homework, time to come inside. It is called growing up. Most of us can remember these moments in our lives, but forget what was before that time. Why you may be asking?   Because this was our 1st responsibilities in life. Think about that for a moment. It also is a very important part of our lives because this is where we begin to get book knowledge from starting school. Just another method of learning but it is where we got a different kind of encouragement. This is where we learning the basics of grammar, writing, math, even history and much more. From kindergarten to middle and high school this is the basic knowledge that most everyone has vastly available to them.

But who encourages us to keep that magical side of knowledge growing? The side that makes us hold onto hope and faith in the unseen and maybe even unheard? The encouragement that helps us continue to develop the basic explanation of what I call advanced intellect of your Psychic Awareness.   Sometimes even in basic school settings a Gifted child experiencing things other than what is taught from a formed educational outline can get easily labeled as Weird, Slow learner, Daydreamer, even forms of Attention Deficit. Let me share with you a personal story of something I experienced.

Whenever I went into a new environment I had a fear of what the place was going to make me feel like. My defense was to TRY to shut it out or off. Remember I was hearing people who I couldn't see at the time even in first grade.

You may find this funny, but me not knowing what to do to make the voices go away I would repeat the same words in my head . "Please stop, not now, I don't want to hear you." You will never guess what happened next? I actually lost part of my hearing when I really tried hard to block it out. The teacher asked me if I had a problem hearing and of course I said yes.

I was Immediately sent to the nurses office thinking maybe I had a blocked ear or a ear infection. Then send home, off to the doctors.   The Dr couldn't find anything wrong. So being cautious the Dr. sent me to a specialist for Ears , Nose and Throat . I remember sitting in the booth doing the hearing test saying in my mind, please let me hear these beeps. I did and they found nothing wrong with my hearing.

This was how my body and mind adapted as a child to hearing voices that were overwhelming. My own way to shut it off, at the cost of not being able to hear normally as well.   I learned very quickly I had to deal with this a different way.

I also had issues with breathing and hives with no medical explanation for it happening.   All during a process as a child trying to close off a VERY strong part of who I am. Can this happen as a adult? Absolutely. It can cause us Stress, Paranoia, and also Phobias to name a few.

A lot of children and adults end up on some type of medications to try to help these anxieties. I get asked a lot if being on certain medication can alter your abilities?

I can honestly say I have found they really do not, if you want to learn. Sometime they can help. I would never suggest going against any doctors prescribed treatment plan. In my opinion if you want to expand your gift it will happen no matter what and this is why...
Most people are so attached to their own ideas, desires, and LEARNED processes in society, that they are unwilling to consider any messages but those methods. But it does not mean they are not receiving it.

  Most of the time you already are receiving these messages or feelings, but do not recognize it. But it is possible to open up and learn to recognize these communications either coming from listening from the inside of yourself, others, objects, nature, different locations the list goes on and on but it starts with improving your receptivity. I will keep repeating what are people like when you listen to them from the inside? Because it truly starts with you.

So what is the feeling, inside most people?   Inside most people is a feeling of being separate. Separated from everyone in their own ways. You are not! We are or can be apart of everyone and everything. There is a spot in the front of your forehead that many psychics and paranormal sensitive's call your 3rd eye. This is where I have found most people have a block or almost a shield because they do not want to believe what they are receiving or feeling or just to busy to pay attention. There are other spot in your throat that hinders your words from flowing freely, over your heart that, if have had your heart broken can cause you to stop feeling purely and

openly. This also includes your gut instinct or just instincts
in general that we tend to tone down and "Not Listen" It all starts by slowing down.

One of my favorite quotes is by Albert Einstein -

"When Technology has passed Humanity , it is time to go back and feel again."

This says a lot from a great man that did not have a quarter of the technology we have today.

My grandmother use to have a picture of him that no one ever saw, until after she passed and I found it. I wondered why did my devout Roman Catholic Grandmother would tell me daily "Never let anyone tell you what you have is not a gift, it is a gift from God and all that is or has been".   Than I thought to myself "Is this a message from her?"

So, I decided to do some research and a bunch of his quotes showed up, on my now ancient computer.

This is the one that jumped off the page at me.   I felt it was a message from her, which is why I am sharing it with you.

It was a message, so is anything you feel. These are small visible messages we miss, maybe while cleaning out a deceased love ones items like I was.   I could have just thrown that picture away. But I didn't. I listened to myself and said why?

You have to start by listening from the inside of yourself to make this process of self development work ...No matter what that Gift maybe.   I am talking about you.   If you decide to take it one more level and open up, this book can help everyone .Even family or your own children to better understanding what it is you and they are feeling.   Even the paranormal investigator can use my book to hone in on a sensitive level.

I would really like for you to embrace your gift. It is enough for me. Once you accept this aspect of yourself, you can expand your knowledge of be aware of the physical things going on around you that actually could be more by ...." Listening from the Inside" and learning to trust what you feel, without a doubt.

Just because you are a sensitive, does not make you a psychic or a medium. Please understand this clearly. Sometimes saying or even admitting you may be a sensitive out loud or to another person is the scariest thing. Especially for me when having this gift was not as open as it is now. I said before that I feel that everyone is born with a gift.

It can be many things other than having psychic abilities. That is why there are naturally born Psychics, Intuitives and Mediums and then there are trained/studied ones who are Sensitives and Intuitives.   Both I feel are talented in their own way. This goes for your gift as well. Just like dancers use muscle memory to remember a movement, and as the old saying goes once you learn to ride a bike you never forget. Its all Memory. YOURS!! It is inside you just waiting to be unlocked.

NOTES

Chapter 2   ~ Grounding~

Grounding is a very important part a daily routine that I do even today. Sometime when I am at a event or have a lot of clients back to back I will even excuse myself for about 5 minutes and go somewhere, preferably outside and Ground.

Grounding is a procedure that I have grown up with and has helped me in many situations. Including when I do Ghost investigation with a Paranormal Team that I belong to.

It is something that brings you to your center and helps you make sense of many things that you may be feeling at one time. Grounding actually works as a filter to slow things down to a pace that my body and mind can understand.

Have you ever gone into a building and almost felt dizzy from the moment you walked in? This is very common of people that have Gifts or that are Sensitives. The reason we feel this way is because we have no filter to block out what we should or shouldn't be feeling. For me it was visiting an antique store for me to realize I had no protection or control of my senses or intuitions.
The feeling I got was almost overwhelming to and the only thing I could do was actually fall to my knees.
Once I had my hands and feet on the ground of the store I was able to pick myself back up and walk outside.

I remember immediately going to a patch of grass and sitting down on the grass. Fortunate for me it was a nice day out and in the summer. I remember closing my eyes and feeling the sun on my face and I had my hand in the grass feeling the blades of grass under my hands. I felt a slight summer breeze. Most of all I remember feeling completely at ease because I was sitting on the ground. This is where I came up with the method of Grounding. Now am I the first one to ever come up with this? Absolutely not, but it helps in so many ways that to this day I do it daily. This is the first thing I teach anyone who I mentor or who takes a Psychic Awareness class with me.

Grounding is a form of connecting yourself to the earth. To firmly know that your feet are planted on the ground and you are in control. Please remember those words when practicing your Grounding method.

This is something that can take 5 minutes to add to your daily routine as you develop your Gifts.

After a few days it does become habit and like me you will be able to feel if you need to redo it. Sometimes Sensitive people or people that have Gifts tend to become somewhat afraid to go places. I don't want to say antisocial because if you were to go into your own home you would be more than happy to visit and socialize.

But going to the Mall, Grocery shopping, any place that has a large amount of people and energy that you may not be comfortable with can make you almost physically/Emotionally Sick.

Grounding will help you feel more secure along with Shielding that I will explain in the next chapter so you will be able to know you can experience all the above and know you have a filter that helps you to "Listen from your Inside" on exactly what if anything you are to hear!

When choosing an area for grounding in or around your home, make sure that you have no electronics going and just for 5 minutes you are taking time to commit to practicing your Ground Technique.

If you are able to go outside then I highly suggest that you do. You will be doing this lesson barefoot so make sure your spot is a spot that you feel comfortable taking your shoes off in. I am going to explain this method first if you are outside and secondly   if you have to do it inside your home or place of work.

Once you have your spot picked simply take off your shoes and walk around for a moment in the grass. Think of all the things you have to do today, tasks you may have to do at work, even what you may have to do after you are done with the Grounding. Let your mind slowly quiet down. Once you have felt your mind slowing down very simply allow yourself to feel what you are doing. How does the grass feel on your feet? Is their a breeze? Can you feel the sunshine on your face? You now are in the right mind and body set to start your grounding. Wiggle your toes slightly and feel the grass on the ground. Feel your connection to the Earth. If you need a visual, think how everything around you including yourself is planted firmly on the ground because of Earths gravity . Bring everything in to your zone as a connection. Can you Smell flowers? Do you hear any familiar sounds in your area you choose? These are all visuals that only take moments for you to connect with. But because we are so busy multitasking we sometimes forget to stop to smell the roses.

Once you have all of those feelings and sounds in tune with you. Feel the strength of the Earth and the softness of the grass on your feet. Let that feeling surround you. Take a few deep breaths in and out and you are done! You have successfully done a grounding.

Now if you cant get outside you can also ground inside your home or even at work. With this you want to make sure if possible that you can be somewhere again where there are no electronics going, where a phone or text message won't interrupt you doing your grounding, and also make sure no one, even pets will bother you for just 5 minutes!

Try to go near a window. Again be barefoot.
Sometimes it does help to be able to recall a memory of when you were outside . A lot of people have a very strong connection to the Ocean.
When they first put their feet in the edge of the water the feeling almost is refreshing and soul fulfilling. If you have to visualize yourself in your spot outside but actually being inside, these visuals are extremely helpful.

I often do this at Events when I can not get outside to ground but I can take 5 minutes to find somewhere quiet and do a inside grounding, that takes just a little bit of your imagination.

Again what you will do is start thinking about all the things that are overwhelming you at that moment. Let your mind process it. You will feel yourself actually slow down because instead of fighting it you are accepting what is making your feel not grounded. Once your thoughts have quieted down, start to see what is around you. If you are at home inside, is it raining out? Can you hear the rain on your roof? Is it windy out? Do you see leaves blowing around? When you look at the sky from your window is the sun trying to peek through the clouds?   Make a connection to everything you are seeing at the moment .

Pick your foot up and actually feel how hard it is to stand on one foot for a moment and then place it back down.

That is your connection to the Earth and gravity centering and Grounding you. You are done. This Grounding Technique can be done just about anywhere! It just takes you to slow down your thought process and "Listen from the Inside" What you should be feeling and not everything coming at you all at once.

It just takes a few moments no matter where you are or what you are doing to Ground yourself so that you can feel more filtered by the Intuitive feelings you may be having coming at you .

I always try to keep some sort of notebook even if it is a little pad and paper in my bag. If I ever feel overwhelmed in a location and feel the need to leave or even get outside and re-ground myself. Make sure you make a note of it . Make a note of the time of day, and your location.

Later on you can even convert that to your Journal and possibly do further research as to why you felt that way , at that moment.

That is one thing that I would highly suggest, that is starting a journal. I have one by my bed, one I travel with, and one in my studio where I do Readings from. I also have my famous sketch pad and pencil I bring with me on Investigations. They cost next to nothing and it is good to keep notes on your personal journey while going through this process of Listening from the inside and getting more in touch with your Personal Gifts, and developing them to whatever goals you would like to see them grow to.

One thing that I will include at the end of this book is my email address. I tell each of my students that I mentor or anyone who takes my class I am available to discuss your progress or to share your Journey with me . This does include anyone reading my book. Just remember please be patient with me returning your emails.
I do not have anyone who answering emails for me. I do this all myself, and I will within 48 hours reply to your.

Another book I am working on is sharing personal stories with permissions of my clients and students. Expressing what having a reading, taking my classes, having me as a mentor, or reading my book has done for them. I do hope to hear from some of you as well.

<u>NOTES</u>

Chapter 3 ~
Protecting yourself & your Energy

Protecting yourself is so very important to safe-guard you and your Gifts. It does not matter what you believe in as long as you draw your protection from someone or something. I will give you a few examples of different ways to add protecting yourself into you routine as well.

This can be universal for anyone really. I believe when our loved one's or pet's pass over they become Guardian Angels to not only you but others in your family. This is why many Psychologists cannot rule out the fact that children are innocent and sometimes can see the other side and passed on loved ones they may not have even met in their lifetime. I will go over a technique to work with your children to see if this is true in your own life later in the book.

Have you ever noticed your Pet staring at something invisible in the room? So transfixed watching something that you can't see? Bark at thin air?   I have a Cat that like's to climb an invisible person. Whenever she does that I know my angels are around me. I pay attention to what I am feeling at that moment and may even document the date and time in my journal to look at later.

Whether you choose to believe or disbelieve the concept of protecting yourself and your energy is your personal choice but I can tell you that it does help, because it may be an Energy that you have felt before.

I always draw energy on my Grandmother and actually both sets of my grandparents in some cases. I know their energy from when they were alive and I can stimulate that feeling in my memories. Protecting yourself does not have to be done everyday but I do suggest it at first so you can easily do it before heading out to places that in the past maybe made you feel uncomfortable. Most People with Gifts that I have met usually have a hard time controlling the amount of information you get and when you are receiving it. In the next chapter we will talk about control and trusting what your Psychic Abilities are telling you.

If you do not or can not connect with a loved one you also may use an Arch Angel. There are many books on Arch Angels and also information on the Web too. This time I am going to use my Grandmother and Arch Angel Michael to protect me.

In a quiet place in your home or choosing it is almost like saying a Prayer. But you are asking your love one or your Arch Angel of to give you protection in your daily life while you explore the journey of development with your gifts. I will often use the following Protection Prayer.

But please feel free to add or take out what you are comfortable saying or asking for: " *I humbly ask Arch*

Angel Michael, Angel of Protection to guide and protect me as I go through out my day . I am developing myself to better understand my gifts. I ask that you send me just enough protection so that I may continue to learn and grow with your guidance and blessings. " Make sure to follow it up with "Amen" or "Thank You"

Another Protection that I use a lot is the Lord's Prayer. The paranormal team I work with does this before we enter into any dwelling we gather as our group and bow our heads and say this prayer or another out loud. Depending on your Faith you may be comfortable using this method or choose not to. It is entirely up to you!

"Our Father who art in heaven, hollowed be thy name. Thy Kingdom come, thy will be done on earth as it is in heaven. Give us this day our daily bread and forgive us our Trespasses as we forgive those that Trespass against us lead us not into temptation, but deliver us from evil.)

...

Again it is important to show respect and also Thanks for any Blessing that is bestowed upon you . So whatever you are comfortable saying "Amen" or "Thank You" Just please remember to close with one of them.

Sometimes saying a Prayer or asking for a Blessing out loud is so important. I sometimes gives you that extra boost to feel like you can do this . I have often said that I believe in everything . Everything has Energy .

I also believe in many different forms of protection no matter what your Faith maybe.

Once you have said your Prayer or Blessing the next step is very much a visual of using your imagination. I have said that when we are children the possibilities are endless because we use our Imaginations and have endless hope and faith. If I am sharing my knowledge with you properly in this book, you should start to see a pattern developing. It is using something that you used as a child and then you started growing up and this is where sometimes there is a Blockage or Stop in your development of your Gifts that you were born with. Not knowing maybe until now, doing these mental exercises is slowing without you feeling it or actually stressing it, taking down that blockage! So if you are good with using your imagination I would like you to draw on that and add what I call "Psychic Shielding"

I was taught this by my second mentor at a time that was so very difficult for me. I had lost my Grandmother, and I was going through a divorce. My point to this ....we all have personal baggage, drama and issues that we each deal with on a daily basis . No one should be telling you how to deal with your issues . This technique actually gave me the added courage to get done what I needed to do and move out of what I will call my "Psychic funk" . I can laugh now about It but, it was not fun then.
This is called Psychic Shielding. This does work very well once you commit to doing it. What you are going to do is to pick your favorite color or a color that you can easily recall clearly in your Minds eye. Your Minds Eye is the spot in the middle of your forehead that Psychic and Holistic healers call your 3rd eye Chakra . This is where many of you will see and feel one or many of the Clairvoyant Gifts you may have. I have all of them and use them daily. I am a Full-Time Psychic Medium. I use

a lot of examples when I mentor and each person is different . But I try to use Universal examples so you get a general idea of what I am trying to teach you .

I think everyone in the world has seen the movie "Dirty Dancing" with Patrick Swazye . If you haven't I am sorry as it is an iconic movie of our generation. In one scene Johnny (Patrick's Character) is teaching Baby about frame work . If you can recall the movie, he holds his arms up and says " This is my dance space, and this is your dance space."   He almost creates a semi circle in front of him. What we are creating now is your Psychic Space that once in place will help filter out what is and isn't important while learning about "Listening from the inside"

You now are going to take that color you chose , Mine is lavender. While standing very simply imagine that color surrounding your entire body. You can make your circle in your Minds Eye as close to your body or as far away as you like. I usually hold my arms out in front of me and physically create a circle. If you like you can also hold one of your arms up and think of a real Shield of Armor on your arm. Whatever images work with you use them!

This Circle you just created is surrounding you in the color you chose . Make sure it goes completely around you and also under your feet. You are creating a bubble almost . If you have to recall the shimmery colors of a bubble. This is what is now around you. It may only take you a few seconds to create this Shield but it truly make a huge difference in your gaining control and opening up for more than you may have even expected with your Gift.

I would like to explain how Psychic Shielding works . By creating a shield around your body you can now feel in charge of what is coming through like adding a Toning System to your body. This shielding will help you because most of the people I have mentored have shared what they experienced when they have their shielding around them.

Almost everyone experiences a sudden flash or vision of the personal color of their shield. It almost acts like a alarm system but one for your body! When this happens take a moment to look around. Take note on what you are feeling. Where are you? Who is closest to you? What time is it and date?

What do you do if you are in a situation that you just can't process the Transmissions you are receiving? Push it out through your Shield and just think of that strong color you chose all around you. The power of Intentions to adjust your Psychic Volume to a comfortable level and most importantly an enjoyable level by simply deciding to become less aware.

I use this Psychic Shielding a lot when going to new places that I am unfamiliar with. Also every single time I do a paranormal investigation with the team. You have to remember one very important thing...If you do Ghost Hunting you are your main tool used in the investigation. Every thought, feeling, sensation you get is just as good as any high tech piece of equipment used normally on a Investigation. Which is why even if you do not investigate its just as important. Its your personal Security Blanket filled with your energy and nothing can get through your shield without giving you a flash warning!

As you adopt these methods into your daily routines, you will immediately find yourself knowing when, where and how your receiving psychic information. Another very important step to being able to control your Gift.   If you journal your data it will help to develop a trust In yourself and also validity of your psychic impressions.

NOTES

Chapter 4 ~ Identifying your Gift~

I can honestly say that there are many, many types of different kind of Gifts each of us may have. They may not even fit into one category or another completely with the way that I am going to describe them. The one thing I would ask is that If you connect with any of them in Full or Part it is so important for you to learn as much as you can about it. This book is just part of the tools that you can use to connect and learn about YOU!

It was not easy when I was researching this information almost 22 years ago now. Computer technology was not what it is today. But I can say I met some very Unique Psychics, Mediums, Gypsy readers, Astrologist, Numerologists, and my list can go on and on. I did find back then by experiencing different lectures, and classes that did help me to learn not only about the Gifts that I possess. Now over twenty years later, has helped me to guide many others who have come to me to help them. They learn to identify develop and control their personal Gifts as I support then while they go through what sometimes is a very emotional Process.

Sometime when you finally meet someone who is genuine about wanting to help you and is not looking to make a fortune by mentoring you it can be a real game changer in your life.

I can remember many students almost breaking down in tears because they felt they could finally open up and talk freely about their life experiences, both good and bad with someone who actually believed them.
This is how much my Mentoring and Passing on My own legacy to others effects me. On my Website it does say $50 for a hour of Mentoring with me. Money is not important when I truly get someone who I honestly feel will take the tools and Yes sometime homework and make it work. Not just come to me and talk about what they have but also truly learn from one another. When I meet people out at an event or get an email, I will actually reply with do you mind if I call you? Once I have spoken to them and their have been many, and most will tell you I did not take a penny for helping them Find the right methods to assist them to open up Listening from the inside.

I know how much some Psychic or Psychic Educators charge to get a Certificate or even learn in a group setting. I do this personally one on one. Or even through Skype or Facetime for those who do not live around me. Do you know what I ask for? I if you live close by I like to let people with gifts come to an event and help by taking appointments, or bring them with me and have them read Tarot cards if that is their thing. This helps me and also builds their own self confidence. When we do this you get the chance to see others and realize just how far you have come. If you do not live close by I may ask for a nominal fee.   Seeing this growth in my students, I think sometimes they do not even know how happy it makes me on "MY INSIDE" and also they see they are not alone!

Developing and identifying your Gift really begins with listening to the still, quiet voice inside of yourself. If you feel you identify with any of the names of different categories of Sensitivity make a note of it in your Journal and I suggest after you are done with my book to find more ways to increase your Self Awareness. Along with continuing to repeatedly practice what I have shared. There are many different people who may already know that are have a gift but are you a Empath? I am and until I was about 22 yrs old I never knew it. So this is where I would like to start because it can effect you emotionally where you may have someone telling you " Your just too Sensitive,"

Empaths - Are people who have the ability to sense the feelings and thoughts of another person. They are naturally tune in to the energies around them. This ability comes with a positive and a negative side.

If this describes you, the positive side is you are a great listener, and compassionate to the needs of others. If you ever find yourselves in a disagreement with someone you do your best to find a way to resolve it as quick as possible and try to avoid confrontations with others who may cause them. Empaths are in touch with their own emotions and are able to express their feeling well, if they have not shut them down due to being pegged as the over sensitive one. Most are also non-judgmental and have an accepting nature .

Empaths need alone time each day. They can be social and expressive in their thoughts and feelings. However, they can also be reclusive and isolated almost afraid to say what they feel. Many Empaths find it difficult to be in crowded or extremely noisy places because they feel the energies so acutely, it overtakes their central nervous system and create almost a panic attack.

You will find if you are an Empath that you love nature as it helps to release all your pent up emotions and gives you some quiet time to recharge your internal batteries . Pets also offer a source of comfort   as they offer unconditional love and people who are Empaths do very well when they are around this type of honest energy.

Empaths have a natural way to sense others emotions without them saying a word. A good example is a Mother can look at a child and without them saying anything and know they do not feel well. Or you can look at a co-worker and tell if they are in a bad mood because of the vibes they give off. Another good example is when your phone rings you can answer the call and with just the word "hello," from the personal calling you. You know something is wrong.

I am sure some of you are shaking your heads right now agreeing that you fit into this category. Most Sensitive are Empaths. It is something I have learned through the years and also meeting many other Psychics and talented

Mediums and Readers all over the world we all share this quality.

Most professionals even experienced Empaths have a hard time controlling what they feel in extreme situations.

THE DOWNSIDE- Empaths tend to take on the lower energies of those around them. After being in a crowded public place they feel irritated or out of sorts with themselves and not exactly sure where it came from.

After being with someone who may be having a hard time emotionally with a situation in their lives they can also take on some of that depressing energy . The reason is because they want to fix it or always want to do more to help and sometime you know you just can not help them. It can be extremely draining on Empaths emotionally and mentally. It is always important to remember that the best way to help someone is by staying positive yourself. If you join the other person in their Misery you now have 2 people that feel bad. Is this natural? Of course everyone has EMPATHY but if you are an EMPATH It can be depleting of your energy. The best way you can help someone is by not getting caught up in their illusion or drama. Stay in your positive space and be a role model for them. This w ill help them much more than connecting with that lower energy of someone who is having a hard time.

This is where Grounding and Shielding come in to protect yourself from the negative side of being an Empath.

The "Claira's" -

Know your psychic channels of communication. We often think of a "Psychic Skill" as being the ability to see mental pictures or "clairvoyance". However, seeing is only one means of receiving information. This can be like a movie playing clips in your mind. This is how I see them, short images of people I may not know or someone who is no longer living. This is a skill I use every time I do readings, also when I am on an investigation with my team the "Extreme Paranormal Encounter Response Team" EXPERT.

No, we are not experts as there are not experts in this field. Only people that have many years of experience that have tried and failed and tried again to succeed. It's called trial and error and I would suggest you get used to it. Making mistakes is part of it. But I do not consider any part of it a mistake, if you learn from what you did.

"Clairsentient"-which is the ability to get your information through feelings. This is normally the first one people recognize because it is a feeling that can comes from nowhere. You can use this to personally better understand what you are feeling and know it may not be your own feeling, but that of a loved one who has passed or even someone you may be standing next to, or even your location.

Does the location have a history? This is all stuff that you will be doing to confirm what you are feeling is true. Almost like a detective or Ghost Investigator. To truly develop your Clairsentient, it takes you to be willing to put the time in to follow up with what you feel.

"Clairaudience"- which is the clear hearing of a voice Inside or outside of your mind.

This is where we start by Listening from the inside, to try to recognize your personal gifts. Psychic's, Mediums, Readers, Paranormal Investigators, and Sensitives rely on and sometimes do not even know they are using, is this Clairaudience.

It is very hard to trust today what we hear because of all the noise going on. Not only around you but inside your head as well. You must learn to truly hear yourself and eventually block out all the other noise but that of what you are trying to hear.

It is the reason Paranormal investigators do not allow anyone else to bring electronic devices inside their investigations. It causes noise clutter and can affect the true sounds of what you should be hearing. All phone are either shut off or put into airplane mode for this exact reason! Experiencing Clairaudience can be a true "ah ha" moment in your life! Just imagine how much more you can receive once you personally identify with one or more of these clairvoyant gifts. I am excited for you because it is how I felt when I had my "AH HA" Moment .

Now come one of my favorites and also I think one of the hardest ones for a person who is developing their gifts to actually trust and have enough courage, and strength in themselves to share with others when it happens.

Claircognizance- Is the ability to know entire chunks of information about various subjects without knowing how. Not having any prior knowledge of the subject. This can be very confusing for the untrained but not impossible.

How you develop your awareness and approach your skills depends on how you practice and how strong this Claira gift Is for you. How can you get entire chunks of information if you have never gained this information yourself? That is the amazing part of this gift. You do not need to know prior to the moment you receive it. But once you receive it research the subject and prove to yourself that the information you just received out of nowhere is true or not true. Don't be afraid to make mistakes!! I still make them today but I do not want to hold back my progress because I was afraid to speak up and say exactly what I felt, Saw, Heard.

Medium- Having a Medium Gift does not necessarily make you a full Medium. Being a True Medium is having the ability to raise the vibrations in either a reading, Investigation, or a home to hear messages from both this world and the next. And having the ability to connect with
THOSE WHO HAVE PASSED AND RELAY THEM TO THE LIVING.

One thing I would like to point out that is so important. Talking or communicating with the Dead even if you are trying to contact a loved one is not recommended unless you have many years of experience and learning . It is not a game to play among friends or something that is performed at a bachelorette party for fun.
This is something that can put the untrained person danger. If you feel you have a Mediumship gift you can

acknowledge it but you should seek someone around you to personally mentor or take you under their wing and guide you to understanding the full strengths and also how it can weaken you if you are not protected. I myself have helped other Mediums develop their Gifts but it must be done in a protected and safe environment and even then certain precautions before and after must be followed.

There is a old saying in the Paranormal Investigation World every time we put ourselves in a position that we communicate with the Spirit World. It doesn't matter who or what your ability , or time in the field, etc.....
  Paranormal investigator , Empath, Intuitive's , Psychic, and Mediums all know this and so should you if you plan on developing this skill more. "It isn't a Matter of Time , it is a Matter of When!" Something may go wrong or attach itself to you. Even the best of us have had it happen. Including me!

Most investigators and Psychic/Mediums like myself know that this is FACT! Even people like myself have experienced something so horrific. It is what made me many years ago want to learn what exactly I could do with my Psychic/Mediumship abilities to help others, find answers and also try to help people that may have gotten themselves a Paranormal Problem.

But is does take a lot of trust of the people you are doing this with. I wouldn't be doing what I do if it wasn't for a wonderful team that knows me, knows my body language and also can tell by my action if I need help. This is on the Paranormal investigating side of being a Medium. But so important for everyone to understand. Because of all the Paranormal TV shows on now it is very encouraging sometimes to get people to want to venture in this field. Please trust your instincts , and "Listen to your inside" if it feel wrong it probably isn't the right path for you!

More things that may have happened to you to make you think you may have a mediumship Gift is the ability to connect with a loved one that may have just passed. Feel them around, maybe even smell their perfume or cologne they used, See a shadow and feel like you are not alone.

Having the blind ability to walk into a building knowing nothing about it and being able to tell if their was a fire, flood, a death or even in worse case, a murder.
You get a feeling as if someone is watching you and you feel like a presence is trying to communicate not by your choice but because of the overwhelming feeling you are getting through you Gift. It may be strong and overwhelming enough to have to leave. This is something that you learn to control more as you develop your gifts.

There are other fancy names that people have come up with to describe the same abilities that the "Claira" descriptions that I listed for you .
Some of them you may have heard of or not. I try to keep It very simple when I am teaching and the more you develop that is when you can better label the gifts you may have.

Psychometry - Is the ability to touch a item with your hand or even hold it up to your 3rd eye area and receive an array of knowledge from just touching or holding. This gift allows you to know great details about the item. Like the location where it came from. In whole or part many details of the life of the person it belonged to. Just like a Medium can connect with pass over people, In Psychometry you are now connecting with a object.

Psychometry is something I have, remember I mentioned in another chapter about my visit to an antique store. Before I was able to control it, it was difficult. With Grounding & Protecting it does tend to filter these things out for someone who thinks they have this ability and can not control it, and I shared what happen to myself while I will still learning as well.

Today I can with certain amount of preparation now go into an antique store. But I will not touch anything or I will start to connect with the item. Usually if it is winter I can get away with wearing gloves so I can briefly look at a item . BUT if you live in a warmer climate than Upstate NY you may not own or would look a little odd if you were to wear them. Simple solution I use during the summer is ask someone who is with you to pick the item up and show it to you.
I will even ask my husband, friends or family does it have
        good energy? Sometimes I forget not everyone can do this particular thing I can. But it does help to be prepared for it. Another example is reading or picking up information on a House or Building by touching a Wall.

This is something many people have seen me do when I do investigations.

Extrasensory perception-   I think is a very funny one and believe we all have a sense for it. I don't think you would be reading my book if you didn't. This is a form of ESP or 2nd Sight, and a Sixth Sense. Well honestly I don't think I need to explain this one as there is many EXTRA SENSES not just a SIXTH as those I listed above.
It doesn't matter if you feel a connection to one of them or many of the names I have listed above . What is important is now you are taking a step in the right direction in development by gaining knowledge about these different types of abilities.
Can you have more than one? Yes
Can you have all of them , YES.
BUT it makes it incredibly hard to develop them until you learn to tone down one while you learn another. It is not impossible because I am walking proof YOU CAN!!

But this does require patience and time . Lets face it many of us are very impatient and want to know how to instantly be successful using their talents. It is very normal but you do have to take it slow and like I said. Pick one at a time and develop it until you feel comfortably able to control it. Sometimes having control will help you learn a lot easier the next Gift you have chosen on this list that you identify with.

There are many Psychics, Researchers, Paranormal Groups, that have their own names for each of these gifts.

Which is why I took you to the basics of defining and naming them. Before I actually admitted I was a Psychic Medium I use to say I had a Gift and a Curse. The reason was Control and I had none and I am not ashamed to admit it. I am proud to say now I do and so can you.

Some of the Methods I used will be coming in the next chapter or Two along with Developing the skills you gain from "Listening from the Inside"

<u>NOTES</u>

Chapter 5 ~ Developing your Gifts~

When I was learning from both of my Mentors as well as learning on my own it was important that I kept it fun. Even now you may be very serious about learning to bring out more in each of your gifts, its very important to me when I educate people on how to do this that it does not become boring or stressful.

Even at Events when I am asked to do a Lecture on different subjects pertaining to Psychic/Medium, not one of my Lectures are ever done the same way. They are different, because each place I go the people are different. I love doing it this way and the people listening to me talk are not just sitting there, they are actively involved!

Different methods work for different people, just like I said each of you are very very special, talented and have your own blue print of uniqueness that is like no other! This is not something to be embarrassed of! Feel proud and Own your Gifts that are a part of what make you, YOU!

Do you want to be ORDINARY? I know I don't.

Once you own that you have an Ability or a Gift it is so empowering! It will help you to develop much quicker than if you didn't claim what is yours. It creates a sort of trust and confidence in yourself. There is a difference between having confidence and having an EGO! (That I will get into a little later in the chapter) which can be harmful to your learning. No room for EGO's, no room for perfection because sometimes you have to repeatedly make a mistake as long as you learn more each time you try.

In this chapter I will teach you how to practice on your own ,with Family, a trusted Friend, Husband, Wife, or your Partner who may be learning along with you. Remember "Listening from the Inside" Is a tool used by everyone to help Open up the Gifts you were born with.

PSYCHIC SYMBOLS - Have you ever experienced an "Aha!" moment or wonder why it feels like you just know something without knowing how you know it? Have you ever woken from a dream only to have the events in that dream become reality during your day? Have you ever experienced a sign so strongly it caused you to change your mind or direction?

All of these moments you've had are part of the incredible world of Listening from the inside to trust your Psychic Symbols and Intuition coming directly from you!

Luckily you do not have to be hit over the head, have a near death experience, or grow up seeing dead people like I did to recognize psychic symbols. Everyone receives intuitive messages; we need only to identify them to appreciate the vast realm of information available to us as you learn to trust your instinct! Being intuitive I strongly believe is part of our birth right.

Tapping into your intuition comes with a price. It causes you to break free from mundane, ordinary life and challenges you to live outside the lines. It creates normalcy out of what is otherwise thought of as different. Owning who you are!
Being Intuitive and developing your Gifts will generate you a longing to follow a path that can lead you to something greater than you ever imagined. Being open to receiving psychic symbols and trusting those messages will definitely change your life.

   Once you become Aware, you will never see things the same way unless you choose to shut it off or turn down the volume on your Psychic Awareness and Gifts which does take practice.
As I have said before I was a average kid and with my Grandmother Ann mentoring me she made me feel no different than anyone else. I was as a teen reading peoples energy around them and hearing messages from dead people. Honestly thinking everyone could do this .... even that young I felt a connection to everyone which is another reason I believe with all my heart we all have these abilities available to us all.
I truly recognized my gifts as being Psychic around the age of 19 and that is when I began to recognize Synchronistic events as more then mere coincidence . I truly started to be tuned into becoming Psychically Aware
.

Years later I turned something I wrote at the age of 19 in one of those composition books that I had into the class I teach now called 'Psychic Awareness'
Awareness is real and it is through symbolic representations that we psychically receive intuitive thoughts, images, ideas, sounds, and feelings on a Physical level too. We just need to be made AWARE of them.

Where Do Psychic Symbols Come From?

Meditating Daily will increase your flow of receiving Psychic Symbols or information. A mere 15 minutes when you wake up and another 5 minutes before sleep, can greatly influence your intuitive, psychic and healing capabilities. The reason is because you are slowing yourself down even for just a few moments a day. If you can not meditate because some of us honestly get so relaxed we fall asleep while trying, there is another way.

Find some type of Zen Music or Sounds that sooth you. Like a thunderstorm, Rain, Waves, forest noises. There are many out there. This can be done anytime of the day but I would suggest it for at least 15 minutes. SIT do not lay down and turn on your music of choice.
You may want to set some type of timer on a phone so that it will awaken you from your Meditative State. Close you eyes and slow down. At first your mind will be

racing, but listen to the music and let it send a calmness
through your body.

At this point you may start to see Symbols. Did someone
from your past just pop into you mind? Are you seeing
Colors? Are you smelling any different Sense? Do you
see yourself or someone you know driving? Make sure
you do not judge what you are seeing just accept it and
remember to write it down.   Colors are very common to
see. Different colors represent different colors in the
bodies Chakra System. If you see a strong color take note
of it and look it up to see what color matches the color
you see?
Seeing one color strongly, may mean you have a blockage
and might be good to do a chakra cleansing or balancing.
Reiki Sessions also help remove these blocks. It is also
important to make sure to see what images or messages
you are receiving right after seeing these different colors.
Everything has meaning and all are messages to you!

Your Chakra's follow the Base of your spine and are
Centered in the middle of your body. From Feet to the
Top of your head and there are 7 essential ones that do
help with Psychic Awareness and development.

  Here is the list of Chakra's and the color associated with
them. This will help identify if you are noticing one color
more than another.
It also may mean that you are drawing a lot of your
Energy and Gift from this area in your Chakra as well!
Please remember everyone is different and in this exercise

if you see any of these colors to trust what your Intuition tells you and Of course " Listen from the inside".

Root Chakra - RED

Your 1st Chakra -This is found near your feet which is why it is called your root Chakra. Your Root Chakra helps when you are grounding as this is the part of your body you 1st will connect with the Earth or Gravity. If you see Red or you have a hard time Grounding yourself it may be because you have a blockage in this Chakra. Or it may be giving you a message that you should re-ground yourself. I would try regrounding first and in your next Meditation session see if you still see this color. Sometimes you have the answer and it could be a message that only you will understand.

Sacral Chakra - ORANGE

2nd Chakra- The Sacral Chakra is the center of sexual energy and found in your Private area to your abdomen area. If you see the color Orange again you may have a blockage or it could be a personal message to you. It also could mean you have a strong sense of Sensuality and you draw your energy from this area of your body.

Solar Plexus Chakra - YELLOW

3rd Chakra- Solar Plexus Chakra is the repository of energy from which the power of life and vitality flow throughout the entire body. This is located right at your root center, your stomach. This is were many people feel a strong instinct from . "Gut Instinct" is another name for it. You should always trust this feeling. If you doubt this feeling then I would suggest a Cleansing or balancing as this is a important Chakra that most Sensitive's draw a lot of their personal Gifts from Internally. So pay close attention when meditating if you see Yellow . It also could be telling you that you need to trust this instinct more!

Heart Chakra - GREEN

4th Chakra -Heart Chakra is in the center of your body and is the center of the Chakra system. It is a link between the lower three chakras and the higher three chakras. Sometimes when we see the color Green It could be telling you to open your heart more to accepting the messages you are receiving. This is also a very common area to have a blockage in because we tend as humans to "Safe Guard" our hearts from getting hurt. Trust what your seeing and listen to what messages follow after seeing this color to tell you what your next step should be.

Throat Chakra - BLUE

5th Chakra-Throat Chakra is exactly where it says it is. This Chakra is tasked with keeping the balance between emotions and intellect. This Chakra sometimes can become blocked or shielded by our own doing or from others. Sometimes because your voice is responsible for speaking from intellect and also from your emotions it can become blocked very easily when you have a gift. From many years of keeping quiet and not acknowledging that you are different and have Gifts inside of you just waiting to come out. Also others telling you that you may be "To Emotional". If you see the Blue color it may not mean you have a block but it may be telling you it is time to open up your true voice to all that your gifts have to offer, without worry what others may say. See what follows after seeing blue to tell you your exact message . Each will be different and may challenge you to become more open.

Third Eye Chakra - INDIGO

6th Chakra- Third Eye Chakra is located in the middle of your forehead and is very much responsible for Psychic Intuition, Visions , and also the Spiritual Center of the body that is strongly related to concentration and consciousness.

This area can be very sensitive to pressure when you are receiving or sharing information with others on a Psychic level.

It also can be the first area you feel like you are receiving a message from when you go to different locations. If you see indigo see what follows but also remember that if you can not see something clearly, understand or even have a problem meditating because of lack of concentration you may have a block in this area.

Crown Chakra - VIOLET

7th Chakra-Crown Chakra Is located at the top of your head your Crown area. This is one of the most important Chakras to have open and ready for knowledge as a sensitive, empath or any type of gift you may have. This is where you will learn to develop your skills from divine information that you are receiving from whom ever it is that you connect too. It could be God, Goddess, a Spirit Guide, a deceased loved one. It also could be a way for you to be able to read a location.

This Chakra Is just as important to keep clear so you can see what messages you are suppose to receive. It is considered one of the most important chakras for Psychic development because its is an important energy channel in your body. If you see Violet when doing this exercise it may be that you are truly open. If you are having a hard time understanding clearly, simply stop and clear your mind before trying again. It can be that simple. If it repetitively happens then I would suggest a balancing and cleansing for you. What is most important is that you will know once you start trusting your intuition as to what exactly each image, color, person, animal you see means. If you saw someone from your Past pop up in your meditation. You may want to reach out to them. You may be surprised to find out they may have been thinking of you as well.

Smelling a certain scent that is familiar that may remind you of a deceased loved one, friend or relative means you may have a direct line of communication to that person on the other side.

If you see a friend Driving and not sure why give them a call and find out if they are planning a road trip . If they are you may want to just make sure to tell them to take their time and be safe.

All of those things I just mentioned could be what they mean, but again everyone is different, this is the way you decipher and understand the Psychic Symbols you just received while Meditating.

Another thing that is very common is to see someone you have never seen before. Some people consider this to be their personal Spirit Guide. Many people I have mentored have different images they have seen from Indians to Angels, they are your personal helpers sending you symbols to not only help you grow in your gift but also help direct you in your daily life.

If you see an animal in your meditation. This could be an animal Guide for you and yes you can have more than one.

One of my Animal Guides is a rabbit. How did   I figure out it was one of my Guides you may be asking? I kept seeing it repeatedly no matter where I went . I loved stuffed Bunnies as a child. I remember at Easter my Father would buy me a Stuffed Rabbit. All of these things while you are developing your gifts you must take into consideration that it is not just coincidence.

My Rabbit Guide acts as a protector to me. When I am driving or in a car with someone else. If I see a rabbit on the side of the road I tell whoever I am with to slow down because a deer will be ahead somewhere. I have avoided many accidents trusting my Rabbit Animal Guide and have many witness to this as well. Meditation works in many different ways just like I gave in detail but also have Scientific proof.

Studies show a definite relationship between meditating and Psychic Abilities. Scientists have observed that meditation synchronizes the wave patterns of the left and right brain. This Synchronization apparently allows free flow of information between sides-from the right side which is considered the Psychic side-to the left where we have our verbal centers.

Imagine all that for just 15 minutes a day?? It works and I will be honest I fell asleep listening to that music when I first started, no shame in admitting something didn't work. How did I fix it? I tried different times of the day until I finally was able to do it. Yes different times of the day really do make a difference. Try it! I still try to do this each day. Remember we are ALL- always learning!

Chakra Cleansing & Balancing -After you have started to make meditation a daily routine to open you channels of psychic and spiritual healing that is specifically designed to cleanse and balance the energy centers of your body known as your Chakras. There are many wonderful books, audiotapes, and classes that can help you learn how to balance and clean your Chakras . Some as simple as adding more fresh food to your diet, eating more veggies and as mentioned above Reiki Sessions or having your mentor do an   Aura or Chakra Cleansing on you. I was doing this before I became a Reiki Master and also doing it on myself by spending more time in nature.

Some people like Reiki Practitioners and Psychics that work with Energy have the Ability to cleanse, balance and align your chakras for you. This is one reason why I became a Reiki Master, it was a service I wanted to offer my clients. Most of the time when I am mentoring someone there is a point that I like to offer this service and yes I do it for free for them. This step will immediately increase your psychic communication abilities and boost your energy! Remember to write down any colors you see in your meditative state as they do directly connect to one or more of your Chakra's.

***At this point I will bring up the fun old EGO TRAP. By now with all the techniques I have written, you should have some type of increase in your ability and at least are more aware of things going on around you. It is very easy at this point to fall into I have a "SPECIAL POWER" ego trap.

As you begin trusting in your intuition and gut feelings you may start to verbalize "What you are feeling on the inside" and amaze people. It feels really good to finally be able to share with people some of your gifts. Stay humble! If not it will trigger your Ego-self to take over, and you psychic abilities will automatically reduce as a result. I guess this is a way to make people who truly are developing their personal Gifts never to get a Huge ego no matter how famous or infamous you may become.***TRUTH***

NOTES

ORNATE BOWL TECHNIQUE-

Here is an exercise to develop your skills that can be done anywhere. In this method allow your mind to become blank and relaxed as possible. I visualize my mind as a giant ornate bowl, empty and ready for the infinite universal wisdom of my abilities to fill it with answers. Then I mentally ask a question.

For example; What time will I arrive at my destination? Or, What issue does my client who has a 3pm appointment today want help with? These are some of my examples but I want you to use your own.

I stuck in the 2nd one just so you can see that sometimes I even go back to basics no matter how long I have been doing this for. If you have a Spirit Guide or Guardian Angel you can even ask them to help assist you in this exercise. Or you can just put the question in your bowl and trust that the highest wisdom applicable will come to you.

You will receive the answer in your mind or body as a picture, feeling, knowingness, or audible words. The key to this part is not to over-think it . This is were you will get frustrated . Very simply ask the question and only allow yourself 15 seconds to see, feel, hear the answer. Do not judge what you see just trust it! Try to record your answer you get each time you practice in your Journal. It helps you to see the progress you make the more you repeat these methods.

Here are some Specific exercises to increase your confidence in your ability to tap into psychic guidance:

Parking spaces in a parking lot. Allow your mind and body to relax and become as open as possible. I like doing this one around the holidays when parking is horrible. Allow your mind and body to relax safely while you are driving, become as open as possible to suggestions from "Listening to your Inside" visualize that bowl but this time your entire body will give you the answer. Take a Few slow deep breaths ...Feel your hands being guided by your intuition. Or, ask your Angels or Spirit Guide to find the empty parking space, and request that they give you signs or directions to lead you there. You will surprise yourself how handy this comes in!

I really do LOVE teaching and when I get to teach my "Psychic Awareness" Class. I like to keep it small (no more than 15 people) so   I can give individual attention to each person.   This one I have never had anyone get this wrong. But I do have a more psychical method for this exercise and can be more fun to practice with a friend. You will notice sometime your abilities will get stronger when you are around other people that have opened their own minds to their gifts or in a group setting of people that are taking the same class as you because you all share a common interest.

I told you I try to keep it fun so you do not lose interest and this one does require a partner to do it with.

Take a bowl right out of your kitchen cabinet. The one I use is completely white and ceramic . You can use anything that you like as long as it is not plastic or metal . Make sure it is something that when you close your eyes you will be able to picture that bowl in your mind. The one I use happens to be a old fashion mixing bowl that belonged to my grandmother.

Next you and the person or persons you are doing this exercise with all pick one item either from your purse, pocket, somewhere in the house. Just remember it has to be able to fit into your Bowl. Get a small plate to put those items you choose on.

If it is only 2 of you doing it make sure you each choose 2. No paper receipts or gum wrappers please. I have had people try many things, you can only imagine and I know you can!!! HAHA. Try not to make them common items like a penny or change. Be creative but keep the item small enough to fit on a kitchen plate and also small enough to fit into your bowl.

Once you have your items both take a moment to pick up each item and feel it, feel the weight, shape, edges. I even encourage people to close their eyes for a moment and get the picture in their mind while you hold it in your hand. Only do this for about a minute.

Take a cloth or towel and cover the plate up so you can no longer see the objects on the plate. Lets say there is a paper clip, a hair tie, a small bolt, and large hoop earring. Decide who will go 1st . Flip a coin if you have too! Whoever goes first is going to be blindfolded. The other person is going to say you only have 20 seconds to tell me what this object is that I am going to drop into the bowl in your mind. I am going to physically drop it in the bowl on the table but it will reappear as soon as It hits the bottom in your mind. Proceed to drop the item in the bowl. If they are hesitating tell them they are thinking to much and not trusting their instinct or intuition.

This method is designed for you to trust your 1st feeling and say it out loud without hesitation. So what if you got it wrong. I bet you went with the second thought and the item you thought of first was correct you just did not say the 1st impression you got.

I use this method when I am working one on one with people or in small groups. It is a lot of fun and it builds trust within yourself. You can do this as many times as you like just remember keep it fun and always pick different items. As you learn to trust your judgement try to challenge yourself more. Have your Partner pick an item from the plate on the table but this time DON'T DROP IT IN THE BOWL. Instead have the person who is blindfolded put their hand on top of yours with the item in it and the person holding the item clearly send a message to them repeating over and over what the object is that you are holding. Repeatedly say it in your mind and project it to your partner right into their 3rd eye area. If within the 20 seconds they do not come up with a answer

drop the item in the bowl and give them another 20
seconds, but make sure they at least have a guess,
When you hesitate on what your intuition is telling you,
you are over thinking and not using your Abilities. Then it
is just a guessing game. You will feel the difference.
When you get to this point you are true channeling your
senses and developing your skill to listen from the inside
and trust exactly what you hear or see!
Any of these methods that I will explain to you will take
time, patience and repeatedly doing them. At some point
you should not even have to look at this book but to only
refresh your memory on the procedures. But again you
can put a twist on any of these and make them your own.
Im just giving you the tools. You are the one that hold the
key to the magic!

NOTES

READING ENERGY IMPRINTS

This lesson you start by doing it with a partner. It can be done alone in a different part of this lesson but until you get the idea of how to be aware and read energy by starting small and with someone it helps to encourage you and builds confidence in yourself. This lesson is actually in 3 steps and I hope you try all of them and as you get better challenge yourself.

As I have said that everything has energy in it or around it. It effects everyone because we all have sensitivities and gifts whether you are aware or not. This lesson is designed for you to heighten your awareness of Energy Imprints of both living, passed love ones, objects, places, and Energy in the Atmosphere in a controlled and safe environment for you to learn and Strengthen this Sensitivity.

The first lesson is for you and your Partner to pick a room in your home to do this in. Make sure there is places for you both to sit.

In this lesson you want to pick a area that you are comfortable in and inside please. If you are doing it alone it is ok .The thing that you want to remember is the person you start doing this with 1st you want to know their energy like your own. It is always good if you can make it someone who also lives with you maybe a family member.

Just don't be surprised as I have mentioned before if those around you happen to be suppressing their personal gifts they become more active and actually take a interest in the lesson you are doing and want to try.

Family members do tend to carry some of the same gifts but each generation can produce a new strength or intuition. This is a nice way to connect and have openness about something you may have not wanted to share with them before.

Once you have chosen your room make sure there is another room you can go into that is off of that room but where you can not see what they are going to do!

Also try to do this while there is no added noise in the house. If you choose the living room , make sure the TV is not on and your phones are set on off. Both of those items give off energy and you do not want any added energy in the room but what is going to be purposely placed there please.

Complete concentration from both people is needed. But keep it fun too. This lesson always reminded me of hot and cold game I played as a kid. But this time there will be no hints.

Please explain to your partner that they will be choosing 5 items in the room you both are in now but not until you leave the room.

Make sure to ask your partner that when they are choosing the items to touch them all over if possible, actually pick it up and hold it in both of their hands. For at least a minute please.

Before whoever is going first (In the other room) ask your partner to hold out both of their hands for a moment palms up.

Now take your hands and either put them right on their hands palm to palm-or hover slightly over so you can almost feel the other persons energy. It is actually good to try both to test what you feel. Do this for about 1 or 2 minutes. Then proceed to go into the other room and wait for the person who is putting their energy Imprints on the items to come and get you.

Make sure you ask them to actually come and get you because yelling from room to room may scare you while you are going to be doing something to prepare for finding the objects and can break your concentration. While they are choosing - This should take about 5 minutes. You should be almost in a meditative state . You should feel nice and calm. If possible sit and have your hands in your lap with your palms up still feeling that connection when you laid your hands on theirs. Close your eyes can you already see what they are choosing? If you feel yourself getting over anxious imagine the Bowl that you chose in the last exercise. Just clear your mind and see the big Ornate bowl in your mind empty and ready for pictures to be dropped in by your intuition. The items they are putting their Imprints on.

In this method you actually will not be using the method of the bowl but using your hands to pick up on another persons energy. But sometimes if you get to nervous or over think it does help to think of that Bowl of possibilities so you do not over think but trust what you feel.

Once your partner has come and gotten you from the other room ask them to sit down in that room while you locate the objects. This can be fun so please do not take yourself to seriously the first few times you do this lesson.

Once you are ready to start the first few times take as long as you need. Go around the room with your hands up feeling for energy. Some people can feel it with their hands and some people can feel it by what your body is telling you.   Go slowly around the room even pick up a object or 2 to see if you can feel the other persons energy on it . But here is the kicker...you only get 8 chances the first time you do this.

Again do not over think it "Listen from the inside"? What are your Gifts that run through your entire body telling you to go to, let that lead you. You may even get a slight butterfly feeling in your stomach when you find the object that they touched. If you feel it SAY IT!

  Some of my clients have even said they feel a slight electrical charge that makes their hairs stand up on the back of their necks. Whatever you are feeling as you are walking around the room and touching items TRUST IT and say "This is one of them" Say it with confidence!

No matter what level you are at developing your gifts before reading my book, how comfortable you are with your Gifts you have and also the fact that you are now sharing with another person by asking them to help you develop your's   and maybe theirs as well. It is all knowledge and a way for you to learn to read energy Imprints. You may not get it right the first few times. But each time you do this exercise after you have had your 8 chances. Have your partner then go around the room and physically show you the items they picked and have them tell you why if there was a reason they chose them. For just a moment then touch that object and see what you feel? Make sure you Journal or write down what you felt. It may only be that you feel something for a moment like a chill but the more you practice this the better you will get at reading Energy Imprints.

<u>NOTES</u>

Part 2~

Part 2 of this lesson is to actually have a pad and pen or pencil. Instead of actually saying what the object's are, you are going to write them down.

You will follow the same steps as the first lesson except this time you are going only have 7 tries at the objects they choose.

You will still have them pick 5 and follow the same guidelines please. But this time instead of saying them write them down. Trust your hand and the energy in it to guide your writing of what the object's are. You will also ask the person who chose them for you to leave the room while you try to locate the items with their energy imprint on.

You can still go around the room and feel with your hands but I want you to really try to get a clear picture in your mind of what the object is, and write it down. Another way to do this is, after the person who chose has left the room to sit in the same spot they were sitting in before you left the room and close your eyes for a moment and try to see through your minds eye or 3rd eye.

Again let your hand be guided by your gift, ask your guide's for help if you like. You may use any method that we have gone over to help you gain more sensitivity in a controlled and safe environment while you develop your skills.

You really can use all the above then write down your choices. This time again you only get 7 tries and you want to limit the time you have to choose.

Ask your partner to keep time and only allow yourself about 10 minutes to do this. Then have your partner come back in the room when your time is up. This time instead of you telling them what you wrote down. You will ask them to show you the items they choose. You can if you like, ask them "Why?" They chose those items if you think it will help you to connect to the Energy.

Then share what you wrote down. Remember everyone processes these lessons differently and you may want to mix it up.

I simply am giving you pieces of a puzzle to help develop your gifts. It is up to you to make them Fit the way that best works for you!

NOTES

Part 3-

Part 3 of Reading Energy Imprints is kind of fun. At least that is what the people I have mentored have told me when I give it to them for homework! This lesson has a starting way and also a challenging way as you learn I want you to test your weakness and strengths. Challenging yourself will always challenge you!

To Start- You will need a Partner or a Friend but they will not be with you at your house when they are putting their Energy Imprints on the items . So my advise to you is make sure you truly trust who you are asking to come into your home while you are not their. If you live alone very simply ask them over and step outside. Or if you have a friend or family member that again you Trust and wouldn't mind doing this for you. Have them stop by while you are at work or running a errand. If you are not comfortable with the idea of letting someone in your home without you being their you can have someone else be their with them. You also if no other choice is available step outside while they are choosing the items just make sure you do not go inside immediately. Go grab Lunch, Dinner, see a movie as long as you do not try to read the Energy Imprints until at least 2 hours have passed. It is the same concept as in Parts 1 & 2 , the only difference is that you are going to have them pick 10 items . The reason for this is you are going to have them put their Energy Imprints in 2 separate rooms. You can Pick the rooms they will be doing this but just make sure that they understand that they must hold the item in their hands for at least 1 Minute each. 5 items each room. Total 10.

Explain one more thing to them. Tell them you are going to leave an item of your choosing (by the door, on the table) right out in the open. Make it something you have a connection to . Ask them right before they leave to go to that particular item LAST. Have them hold it in their hands just like the other items for at least a minute and then they are done until later.

So either after work, after a movie, etc..2 hours have passed you are going to now test your Energy Imprint skills after time has passed and the imprints energy may not be as strong. There is a trick to this but I am not going to tell you until last.

If you do not live alone you are going to want to ask whoever you share a home with to leave the rooms you will be working in as well as having the electronics and cell phones shut off. No extra noise please.

You truly want to connect to "Listening to the Inside", your inner Voice, Thoughts, Feelings, Intuitions, and Gifts. Once you are ready you now will proceed to get your notebook and go to the item you chose for your friend to hold last.

Pick it up, close your eyes. What do you feel? Write down everything you feel, what are you sensing, does it smell differently? Write it down. When you first picked it up did you feel a slight energy pass through you hand and run through your body? Write it down! This is your gift and you are now learning how to identify how you actually can turn it on when you want to! Without you knowing you are learning some control. It feels good doesn't it?   But your work is not done. Once you feel you have picked up their energy imprint on the item of your choosing start your work. You can as before ask for guidance from whom ever you choose, you can clear your mind using the Ornate bowl, whatever has worked for you in past lessons connect with it now. Let the feeling you felt guide your way. Remember take your time BUT don't OVER THINK. This isn't a game that you are playing hide n seek but a skill you are learning to read other peoples energy imprints. Limit yourself to a hour to do this. If your friend or partner lives close ask them to come back over. Or call them on the phone and give them the results.

Each time you practice this you are actually learning to turn up the volume on your Gifts and Turn it down. For only that time limit that was set for each lesson.

That is the little Trick I was saving for you! But you may have guessed! After all you are gifted .....

Please again as in all the educational tools I am sharing with you do not expect Grand results immediately. But do expect to see improvement, your gifts getting stronger, and also learning to control them.

The next step in this lesson try to have some fun with it. Don't be so serious that its work! Enjoy acknowledging the ability to Listen from the Inside of you and letting your abilities flourish.

This time you are actually going to have to venture out. Ask a friend, family member or even the person you have been working with to try this at their home.

If you haven't been working with the same person through-out these lesson that is even more challenging and I commend you. You are learning to read more than just one persons energy and that is the goal .

Anyone is capable of doing this if they let themselves go and trust the inner voice and feeling . If you think your brain gets involved and I bet you will be wrong every time. So once you have picked a location (please somewhere safe) inside.   This time it is a whole new ball game. Before you were comfortable in your own location and it may have been a little easier to pick up when someone touched and put their Energy Imprints on items that belonged to you. This time while you are at your partners house you will have them pick a room. Once they have done so, you are going to ask them to go around that room just like in the first part of this lesson and pick 7 items of their choosing. These object already have their energy on them but what you are looking for is that feeling of something purposely jumping out at you. Ask them to do the same thing. Hold each of the 7 objects in their hands for at least 1 minute long. Then when they are done they will call you into the room.

The first thing I would like you to do is have your partner sit and you sit next to them and do the Palm on Palm technique. This is a important step as you want to feel their Energy Imprint. Do this for a Minute or so and then begin. You get 10 tries. But this time anytime you want and I suggest after each time you tell what item you picked go back to your partner and have them put their hands in their lap Palms up and you put your Palms either on or just above them and get that connection each time. As you practice this each time you may not have to reconnect with the person. You may just need to do it once. You may once you feel you've gotten better even take this Lesson outside and try it there.

NOTES

Chapter 6 -
Controlling Your Psychic/Medium Senses And Reading

This chapter may have been what you have waited for in the whole book , but I can assure you that each of the chapters before this are very important steps to take to get you more control when you are using your Gifts. Listening from the inside is about all of these, Grounding, Protecting yourself & Your Energy, Identify, Developing, and Controlling. They all play a factor in learning control because you now should at least feel more confident in controlling your abilities. Learning about each is about Controlling them without you even realizing that you were learning it. But I still have some more Lessons, techniques and Practices for you to build your confidence and also develop the Psychic/Medium Side of your Gift in as safe an
environment as possible. Your home!

In this first lesson you are going to ask a friend to bring over a few small object that have special meaning to them. Maybe something that they can fit into their purse like for a example a ring. Always ask the person you are about to read for PERMISSION. This is something both of my mentors taught me and in today's world I do not hear of psychic/Mediums doing it enough. It is respectful even if they are a paying client and you know they want a reading but it also will allow the flow of energy between you the person and in this case, the object to release itself to you of their own free will. I always say the persons name and say before we begin "Enter name-May I please have permission to read for you today? But you can word it any way you wish. Make sure when you take the item to have a tissue or paper towel with you, if they did not bring it in a small box. The reason for this is that the first time you touch this item you are going to want to be ready for what you feel. So please do not touch it with your bare hands before you are ready to start.

The first few times you try this I would like you to ask your friends permission to take the ring (or object) into another room in your home. Make sure it is somewhere quiet, no electronics going . You may even want to have a soothing incense burning in the room you will be doing this from. Whatever room you choose to do this in make sure it is as Peaceful, almost Zen. I always burn a little White Sage and Frankincense before and after each time I do a reading. It not only clears the area but to me because of my Strega and Catholic background it is soothing to me. I would make sure to have Sage for after your friend leaves ready to sage you home. I will get into Sage a little later in this chapter.

A little prep-work before your friend arrives should be sageing , lighting a Incense or candle , make sure no electronics are going, in this case if you have pets you can allow them in the room with you as long as they will not disturb your concentration. You should ground yourself, and also do your protection.

Say your prayer or ask for guidance and Protection from who ever you feel comfortable asking. When your   friend or in my case my clients arrive I am ready to begin. Yes, this is something I do EVERY TIME I do a reading . In my case it usually is more than one a day so doing the cleansing, grounding and protecting clears the energy in my space from the last person I read for and allows for freedom for new to enter.

So now it is time for you to activate all of your Gifts but you are in control, how strong or light the energy is that you are going to allow for your body to let in when you Listen from the inside.

Close your eyes and think of that ornate bowl empty and just waiting for answers to be dropped in. No you may not be asking questions but it helps to calm racing thoughts and allows you to control anything that may be coming into your senses at this time. YES, you can do this at anytime, anywhere!! Your in control and if you do not want to have anything come in just think of that ornate bowl or the bowl you chose from your kitchen with a cover over the top. This does work but it does take some practice. At this time we WANT the bowl to be open so get that picture in your mind clearly please. You are slowing your thought process down and also take a few slow deep breaths In and let them out. When you are ready to begin open your eyes.

Your going to want to have a Pen/Pencil and a notebook with you. You may want to start if the ring is in a ring box just to open it up and look at it. What are you feeling? Don't over think, write it down. What do you see? Are you seeing an image of a person?

Write it down and try to be as descriptive as possible. Are your Claira Gifts now slowly being activated? Are you hearing anything? A whisper of a voice? Even if you can not make out what they are saying just write down woman or mans voice.

Now I would like you to pick up the item and hold it in your hand so you can still see it. Did you get an Energy boost the minute you picked it up? If you did you are Recognizing Energy Imprints!!! Write down what you feel. Try closing your eyes for just a moment. Are you getting a almost movie like image in your minds eye of people or places you have never seen before? This is your Clairacognance kicking in and keep your eyes closed until when you open them you can recall what you saw and write it down. Are you feeling an   overwhelming sense of Sadness? If you are and it is to much then put the ring or object down and clearly say   "I do not want to feel this " push it away and out of your mind. When you are ready pick the item up again and see if it is gone? You may have to repeat I do not want to feel this a few times but this is a simple reminder, YOU are always in charge!

After about 15 minutes put the ring or object down and sit for a moment and make sure you have broken the connection with the object. Sometimes it helps to run your hands under cool water. A lot of my Students have found when reading objects their hands become super hot. The same way my hands do when I am doing a Reiki Session. I do the same thing.

Now comes the hard part ...bur really is it? I want you to feel confident but not conceited. Have your friend either come into the room where you did your reading or you can go out to them. I suggest them coming to you because this is your Zen area in both items in the space and also the calming scents you may have burning in a candle or incense. Proceed to read what you wrote about the object to them. Don't just read the words but recall how you felt when you wrote them. I can bet if you didn't get it all right you got most of it right.

Please ask your friend not to ask any further questions while you are telling them your findings as it may break that connection you have to listening from all areas of your body.

When you are done with telling them what you picked up. Ask them how accurate you were? Ask them to give you details about the ring (or object). The best way you can explain it to your friend is that the piece you just picked up are puzzle pieces and now as you are learning to control and use your Psychic/Medium Gifts you are asking them to put the pieces of the puzzle together for you. Some of your pieces may fit. If you find that there is something that they do not understand that you came up with ask them to go home and think about it for a day or 2 and see if something out of the blue comes to mind.

Most times when I am doing a reading my clients are so overwhelmed with everything that comes through that they do not remember everything I tell them. This is why I take 10 minutes before each reading I do and do this same process. I write things down for them. I let them take it home with them and they may read it a few days later and something will click " I know what Michelle was talking about " I will normally get a text, email or call telling me they figured it out. I want you to allow your friend to do the same.

No matter what you got right or wrong each time you practice this your senses and feeling will get stronger for you. You will also understand you are developing control. Immediately after your friend leaves please take a moment to sage or smudge your home. Remember this please. The item your friend brings may have belonged to a deceased loved one. You may have connected with, and what I like to say is " I want to make sure they take them home with them too".

Sage & Smudging -your home or wherever you are doing this practicing will help cleanse your area of any Energy Imprints both Alive or passed.

Make sure you do the whole house, closets, pantries and make sure that in each room you have a window slightly cracked so as we say "The old energy has a place to leave from. Burning sage is one of the oldest and purest methods of cleansing a person, group of people or space. While Native American sage burning is the most commonly recognized form of it today, it has nevertheless been a shared practice in other cultures too. From the ancient Celtic druids who used sage as a sacred herb alongside Oak Moss for burning as well as medicinal purposes, to the Indigenous Peoples of the Amazon whose PALO SANTO (sacred wood) sage burning ceremonies are still practiced to this day.

You may buy White Sage at any Metaphysical Store . I recommend you getting it in Loose form rather than Sage Sticks because once you use your sage stick ,you should not
be reuse it again for another use. With loose white sage, you can use a burn safe bowl or get a nice Sacred shell that are really inexpensive. The one I have cost about $5.00. Put a small bunch in your bowl and light until it starts to smoke. This you can reuse but you will get use to how much it takes to do your house . Very important make sure you sage yourself as well. Just pass the smoke from the sage from the top of your head over with your hand.

If you are buying in larger qualities sometimes you can find it at a better price online. Just make sure you check out the sellers ratings and store feedback before making a purchase.

One thing I wanted to touch base on was about your pets when you are doing Psychic/Medium practices. Your pet just like they know when a storm is coming sometime can tell when something is not right in your area as well. Make sure to keep a eye on their actions. If you see them acting very out of character stop the exercise and sage. Including your pet too!

The benefits of using Sage- The important health benefits of sage include its ability to improve brain function, lower inflammation, prevent chronic diseases, boost the immune system, regulate digestion, alleviate skin conditions, strengthen the bones, slow the onset of cognitive disorders, and help prevent diabetes. In the older days people actually used Sage as a disinfectant as well.

Many are going back to this method to avoid the toxins and chemicals in cleaning solutions which is why there has been such a higher demand for sage. Even in a pinch you can use cooking sage right from the spice cabinet. I have done it!

Western medicine   published in a 2006   titled "Medicinal Smokes," in the JOURNAL OF ETHNOPHARMACOLOGY researchers behind the study undertook it based on the fact that "All through time, humans have used smoke of medicinal plants to cure illness.

Research has shown that even small amounts of sage, inhaled, can increase recall abilities and memory retention in people. The brain activity also demonstrates increased concentration and focus on a chosen topic, which means that for young people in school or for those in challenging, intellectually demanding careers, adding a Sage burning at least once a week can be a effective brain booster.

For Sensitives, Empaths, Psychics, Mediums , Intuitives, and Paranormal Groups the importance of using Sage has a long history. Burning sage is one of the oldest and purest methods of cleansing a person, group of people or space. While Native American sage burning is the most commonly recognized form of it today, it has nevertheless been a shared practice in other cultures too.

From the ancient Celtic druids who used sage as a sacred herb alongside Oak Moss for burning as well as medicinal purposes, to the Indigenous Peoples of the Amazon whose PALO SANTO (sacred wood) sage burning ceremonies are still practiced to this day.

Burning Sage is like taking an energetic shower, or doing a deep metaphysical cleansing on yourself and the area you are working. Smudging is also another word for burning sage which is used to purify people, ceremonial and ritual space, object's and any tools you may use when you are reading or practicing your skills.

When I buy something from a garage sale or even estate sale before I bring the item in my home I will sage it right outside. I also will do the same when I buy Crystals or even a new tarot deck. The Energy Imprints of others who may have picked them up before you purchased them, you want to get rid of so that they connected with your own energy. Burning Sage or Smudging Cleanses and It banishes negative energies and any energies that do not belong to you. If you have gotten into a disagreement with someone in your home that would be a good time to sage as well!

<u>NOTES</u>

The next step for you to try to actually reading a person. It is very difficult to read for someone you may know because, you may be judged for knowing things about them not on a Psychic Level but just knowing them and things about their life because of you personal interaction with them.

So when you ask whoever you read for a friend, family member or even your husband or Wife. You are going to tell them you will be doing a Limited Psychic Reading on them and explain the following please.

LIMITED PSYCHIC READING- is where you are actually just going to read about how their day was today or the day before. If you want to challenge yourself you can even try using your "Claira" Gifts and give them a reading or prediction on how the next day or week will go for them. But no more than a week . You can tell them they can ask one question as long as it has to do with something that may or may not happen within the next few days. Ask them to please keep a open mind and also ask them if it is ok for you to call or talk to them about the information you gave them during the reading to see what came true and what did not. It actually is not as simple as that ..but I will explain after I go over exactly how you are going to do the Limited Psychic Reading.

Before they come to your home preferably if possible . Do your Routine prep work . Please, please make this routine each time you read for someone. Ground yourself and Put up your Protection. It should be getting easy for you by now and only take you a few moments to do. Repetitiveness works wonders. Cleanse your space and yourself with a room sage and light your candles and incense that create a peaceful space for you to work in.

Sometime during the summer because my home is in the country on 40 acres in Upstate NY in Saratoga County . I like to go outside and do all the above I will still sage my Studio in my home where I read from but I will go outside and let nature ground me. I feel the sun on my face, a slight breeze and I ask God, The Goddess, The Sun, Nature to Protect and fill me with the knowledge I need to help give my clients the guidance they are looking for. This is something you can also do ONCE YOU HAVE COMMITTED TO MEMORY how to do your routine. Once the person you are doing "The limited Psychic Reading" on has arrived bring them into the room that you have previously prepped. You explain if you did not prior what a limited Psychic Reading is and then ask their permission always "Insert Name, may I have your permission to read for you today?" Wait for them to say Yes, then of course be thankful and SAY IT! Depending how you are feeling you may want to ask them if it is ok to touch their hands a moment. This will help you to establish a Physical connection to them but on a Psychic level. Close your eyes, take a deep breath and begin....

Are you seeing Money?   Are you feeling happy, sad or maybe a little drained?   If Drained you may want to tell them to make sure to get a little more sleep this week because your feeling a bit drained. Or you may feel they may be getting a cold? Or even it being a very busy work week. Remember to search your feelings and connect them with the person you are reading for. Just Make sure you do not hesitate on telling them what you feel!

When you hesitate your mind and heart get involved and this is what happens. You get nervous and think what if I say this and I am wrong . What if I tell them they need extra rest this week because it will be a busy week for them and then I find out it wasn't!!!!! SHHHHHHHHHHH yourself and stop if this happens and take a moment to refocus and let what you are seeing, hearing, feeling come out of your mouth without hesitating.

You can judge later in the week when you see how you did. Right now you do not want to let yourself doubt the gifts you have and your ability to control the feelings . This is now activating your ability to listen to the inside of other people! You sometimes just need to quiet your own mind to let it happen.

Speak confidently but also compassionately and let your gifts flow! You should limit your reading to no more than 20 minutes tops. From asking their permission to ending and saying "Thank you for letting me practice my Psychic Gift on you ".

When they leave or if they live with you make sure you have a notebook or your journal near by and record what you told them. They may not remember everything and you want to have this written down so you can have Validation on what you predicted in your Psychic Limited Reading when you check back with them on a set day that you both picked. Like I suggested no more than 1 week please.

Follow through with doing your cleansing of your space and feel proud because the 1st one you do is always the hardest. Do not be disappointed if all the things you said did not come true within a week . Why? Ask them if you can call them in another week and see by any chance with your notes if it did end up happening.

The best way to do a Limited Psychic Reading on someone is to keep it simple. Do not give any extreme Predictions on your first try but if you feel them, after they leave write it in your journal. No matter how long you have been doing reading for Validating your Gifts and Abilities is something you need to hear to build your confidence.

I always tell my clients that once I have read for them, they are a part of my Psychic Family and I would love to hear back from them. I give them my business card that has all my information to contact me. I also will send them a "Thank you" Later again for allowing me the pleasure of reading for them and sharing part of their life with me. You should also always be very thankful no matter who you are practicing on because when you use your gift and they give you permission to do so, they totally open themselves up to you like an open book. Waiting for you to read them.

<u>NOTES</u>

Controlling- If you have noticed I have very rarely used the word <u>Controlling</u> in this chapter even know it is part of what you are learning. You need to understand and once you do,
  it will happen. If you use all the methods I have shared with you, you are already in <u>Control.</u>

You are now able to Ground your energy to keep your emotions and feeling from becoming overwhelming. Your in Control! You are now able to Protect yourself from feeling things both good and bad when you are trying to do your everyday things like Grocery shop or going to the Mall.

Why? Because you are in Control! One of my favorite things to do is when I see one of my clients at the grocery store and they come up and say "Hello" and they sometimes think that there was a reason why they bumped into me ....its almost like an awkward Silence right before I hear ,"So what are you doing , or what is going on ? " I always smile and I am polite because I am just like everyone else, I am not a celebrity and reply "Same thing as you Chicken is on sale this week." Usually I will get a pause and then we both will start laughing. You cant be to serious doing what I do and I will never get a Ego!

I am outgoing and will talk to anyone. If anything I am sometimes shy when I am in company of some well known people in the industry that are Celebrities on TV Weekly. I am known for blushing because I stay humble and no matter where my life takes me I will never change! I hope you do the same. Do not lose yourself but be true to your values and always treat people how you would like to be treated. Words I live by.

The last part of this Chapter is about connecting with your loved ones and using your gifts even if you are not a Medium. I can guarantee your loved ones have already connected with you in one way or another.   But you just were too busy to notice it.

Connecting with loved ones & Mediumship

Everyone has the ability to feel the presence of a loved one who has passed on. You do not have to be a Medium to have this ability. If you are an animal lover and still own pets but have had a pet or two pass they are still with you as well. You just do not notice the signs.

Have you ever woke up in the middle of the night for no reason and felt like someone was their? Shrugged it off and went back to sleep?

Have you ever felt like there was something sitting on the end of your bed? Again Shrugged it off?

Have you ever been sitting in your living room and all of a sudden saw a shadow and turned around to see what was there and their was nothing?

Have you ever misplaced a item that you set down everyday when you come home, Keys, Cell Phone in the same place. Maybe on a table near the door? Then you realized your out of milk and have to run back out . Only to go back to the same spot and can not find your keys? You back track your steps through your house and you might even ask someone to help you look? Then after about 10 minutes you go back to the spot you lay your items everyday and find your keys maybe on the other side of the table under something?

Your so mad at this point because you cant believe you didn't see them when you looked before, so you just grab them and run back out?

Do you have more than normal light bulbs in your home burn out?

Does your Cat or Dog Bark or stare at a spot with nothing there ?

I could go on and on but I know you probably are saying "Yes" how did she know to a lot of the things I just mentioned?

Our loved one or Spirits in general I will call them sometimes do not have control of a lot of energy but they can do small things like burst of Energy to make all of the above happen.

BUT we are so busy multitasking-work, kids, pets, soccer practice, Dance class, Laundry ,Dinner, Dishes, Smart phones, I-phones, iPAD, Kindles, Instant message, Facebook, Facetime, Instagram, Twitter, Alexa that we are always connected to something or other and always doing more than one thing at a time.

So I ask -Do you think you could actually notice any of the above more than just a coincidence because they were so little but have no explanation? At least not until now anyway   In order to connect to them we really have to slow down and set aside some time to disconnect and just "Listen from the Inside and also the Outside"

One thing I would like to make perfectly clear is that if you have felt any of the above and have felt uncomfortable? If it ever happen again in a very loud and commanding voice say " You are not welcome here , please leave!" Remember you are in Control!

So this last lesson is going to test you Control and you limits as well. If you are ready, if not you can always come back to this chapter once you are comfortable with all the other lessons and feel ready to take the next step. You should always go at your own pace.

If you have woken up and felt like someone was their and it has happened more than once . Next time it happens I want you to listen to what your intuition is telling you.

Is it a comforting feeling? Does it seem familiar? If so very nicely say out loud "I know you are there, but I need my sleep please" .

Many times our loved ones will try to contact us while we are asleep because we are at rest. We are not multitasking we are simply peacefully sleeping . So they will wake you up. It could just be a feeling that makes you wake up or you may have heard something. They do this because they know they have your complete attention and you are almost defenseless. This is why I say as long as you are not scared say the above Sentence.

There is a big misconception that our loved ones or Spirits can read our minds. I have 22 years of experience teaching this method and I will say all of my students have found it successful and a start of connecting to their gift of communication or mediumship.

Our loved ones need to hear verbal confirmation from you so talk to them out loud. They will find a way to answer you. Trust me.

The feeling of someone or something, and I say something because it mostly is a passed beloved pet sitting on the bottom of your bed, kind of a weight? Did you ever have pet sleep their? Say their name out loud and see if the weight moves . Bet it will.

The light bulb's going out is very common in my home. It also has been happening since I was a baby. It was written in my baby book that when I cried and screamed to be picked up, next thing you know a light bulb would go out. Coincidence? Maybe but it still happens today when I get upset.

Does anything like this happen to you? Slow down and think about it. It may not be a light bulb but it may be something else.

Sitting in your living room or any room and feeling or seeing a shadow out of the corner of your eye? But the minute you turn around its gone? Just make a note of it in your journal and any of the examples I gave and anything you think is important that you may want to ask questions about at a later time.

My favorite is the Pets. Staring at wall or looking up in the air, sometime acting up really bad and you have no idea why? If you had another pet that either knew the one you had now they may be seeing them. If it is a new pet the older beloved pet may be trying to get the new pet in trouble by teaching it bad habits . This is so true. I had it happen to me with my 2 yr old Standard Poodle. I knew it was our old dog trying to get her in trouble. So I learned to say out loud " Ginger & Kaos, please stop If your going to teach her something teach her something good"

Just as Stephanie said in her editors notes that night when I went to sleep I dreamed of all 3 dogs playing together and knew in my heart they are still here.

So now I want you to try to connect in a safe environment the room that you have been saging and maybe practicing meditation or you Zen room . A room that you have filled with good Energy . If you do not have a room like this slowly start to make a room for yourself . It doesn't cost a lot of money to bring things into one room in particular that makes you smile, has positive good energy and most of all a room where you can relax and do your next lesson.

In this lesson you are going to only do this for 20 minutes and if it become to much or overwhelming simply stop and ground. You are in control and you can turn the volume down or up on your gifts now when you want.

You will need a candle, (preferably white and unscented) , your note book/Journal, Pen or pencil.
You will start with doing all the prep procedures.
Grounding
Protecting/Shelling/Prayer or Blessing
Cleansing before and after
No Electronics or Cell phones on

Once this is all set you will be finding a comfortable spot in the room you choose and sit. It would be best if the spot you picked was against a wall or somewhere were you had clear site of the entire room.
One you are comfortable, close your eyes and take a few deep breaths in and out and quiet your mind and body and start listening from the inside.
Open your eyes and say, "Now I am ready to communicate (enter name).
You are not going to say anything beside that sentence to start during your session.
From that point on you are going to write down EVERYTHING you See, Hear , Feel , Smell and What your intuition is telling you. Try to stay as still as possible during this exercise.
Do you see the flame on the candle all of a sudden dancing?

Is there a change in temperature in the room?

Do you all of a sudden feel hungry for a old recipe that maybe your grandmother use to make?

Do you have a slight smell of cologne or perfume someone you know use to wear?

Is your leg getting tingly ?

Is the hair standing up on your arms or back of your neck?

Make sure you write all this stuff down, It is important.

Do you feel a slight change in the atmosphere in the room like there is more than yourself their?

Out of the corner of your eye did you see a shadow or an image?

All of this stuff is very common to happen when you ask a loved on to communicate. If you smell a foul smell or hear unhappy noises . Stop your session and say very loud "You are not welcome here . Leave now!" and sage immediately.

Are you feel drained of your energy?

Did you feel a slight brush against your body?

If you have a window in the room did anything odd like a butterfly land on the window.

No matter what you feel, hear, see, smell write It down. Do not Judge what you write , there is plenty of time for that later when your Session is over .

If you know from listening from the inside of you, who this person is by the way things happened? Say hello and thank you for communicating with me today. Limit your time.

When you are done please put out the candle. This candle if you got a big enough one will be the one you use when you practice your skills of communication only. Treat it as a sacred tool to your learning.

Unless you heard any voices this is what I call a communication only session. You are training your senses to become alert to all that is going on in the room you are in. When the session is over, Sage room and yourself and re-ground your energy please. This is how you shut it off and how you learn to Control your gift.

You Practice, learn, grow in a safe closed environment like your home so that when you go out you will notice that your gifts are not controlling you but you are now in control of
them!

This happen's in a very natural way all the lessons in the chapters. How fast you develop is up to you. But I can tell you it will not take you years like I had to go through to get this kind of control. This should help you in Months of practice and pushing yourself just outside of your comfort zone . Not to far, but far enough to challenge you so you are learning.

NOTES

Chapter 8 ~ My Gift to you

I would be honored if I was remember in just a small way by each of you no matter what it is you take from reading my book .

If you notice I left a page marked Notes after each chapter . I did this hoping that you will add your own story after trying my methods in those pages. So if you choose to pass on your own legacy to someone in your family they will have your personal touch to it as well .

You see this book as my Legacy.   I am passing it on to anyone who may connect with it . I do not have any children to pass this on to like my Grandmother did to me. So in many ways each person I mentor I feel as if I did for them what my Grandmother did for me .

At the age of 16 I was told I could not have children. I accepted it and know that my purpose here is not to be just a mother to one, but to many with connecting with you by "Listening From The Inside"

I do have a lot of Nieces and Nephews that maybe someday they will come to me or read my book when they are old enough and say "How did you know this Aunt Shell ?" When that time comes I will be happy to share this with them just like I am sharing it all with you now .

Each of us possess a Gift . I truly believe we are born with this capability . If you feel it and you have children of your own encourage them while they are young to talk about it with you. Keep that part of their minds growing as well as they grow up..

Keep this legacy My Gift to you.   That is not only mine but yours as well to keep growing through many Generations!

Even though I may have not met each of you personally , you are part of my Psychic Family Now. I am always available and one of my Greatest Pleasures is Teaching and Helping.

If you have any further questions regarding this book or if you have any personal experiences you are always welcome to email me and share them. Know you are not alone. There are many of us out their . Continue to keep your knowledge growing . Never stop learning .

My Grandmother use to tell me the day you stop learning , Is when your mind starts dying.

I do plan on writing more books in the future . My goal is to have another book out in Sept 2018. Please go to my website and give my book a review after reading it. Just like with our gifts , "Sometimes we need to have Confirmation ."   I also would love it !

Please stay blessed !

Never stop searching for answers!

Always follow your heart !

Travel as much as possible!

Donate your time if it is all you can offer , it is enough!

And remember , Your blood type is Be Positive so don't ever let anyone dull your sparkle .

Links & Website's

Saratogaspiritualist.com   My Website
Reading are available online, Skpe, Email, Phone, Instant Messenger & Of course in person. Please see my facebook page EVENTS to see if I may be at a event near you or you can also request me at a event by email.   Feel free to contant me on either source if you have additional Questions.
Extreme Paranormal Encounter Response Team (EXPERT) for further information

   Paratalk Radio Hosted by Ted Van Wolf >Mondays 8pm-10pm est. I do a free reading on Air , chosen randomly from the listeners !

   Haunted Hinsdale House >Facebook Page or Search online to visit or Donate to the restoration Project.

   Haunted Bergen House -Information can be found on the Haunted History Trail Site of New York State .

94045534R00063

Made in the USA
Columbia, SC
22 April 2018